ALL ABOARD!

HIGH-SPEED TRAINS

by Nikki Bruno Clapper

Consulting Editor: Gail Saunders-Smith, PhD

Content Consultant: Martin Wachs, PhD
Professor Emeritus, Department of Urban Planning
University of California, Los Angeles

Pebble® Plus

CAPSTONE PRESS
a capstone imprint

Pebble Plus is published by Capstone Press,
1710 Roe Crest Drive, North Mankato, Minnesota 56003
www.capstonepub.com

Library of Congress Cataloging-in-Publication Data
Cataloging-in-publication information is on file with the Library of Congress.
ISBN 978-1-4914-6039-9 (library binding)
ISBN 978-1-4914-6059-7 (paperback)

Editorial Credits
Nikki Bruno Clapper and Linda Staniford, editors; Juliette Peters, designer;
Jo Miller, media researcher; Kathy McColley, production specialist

Photo Credits
Alamy: age fotostock, 5, Bernd Mellmann, 13, Peter Bowater, 9; Dreamstime: Iloveharbin, 15,
Pedro Antonio Salaverria Calahorra, 7, Sébastien Bonaimé, 11; Newscom: EPA/Feng Iel, 1,
EPA/Shen Yu, 21, Universal Images Group/JTB Photo, 19, ZUMA Press/Stefan Rousseau, 17;
Shutterstock: hxdyl, 2-3, 22-23, Oleksiy Mark, cover (train), Petrovic Igor, cover (ticket), tovovan,
train design element, (throughout)

Note to Parents and Teachers

The All Aboard! set explores and supports the standard "Science, Technology, and Society,"
as required by the National Council for the Social Studies. This book describes and illustrates
high-speed trains. The images support early readers in understanding the text. The repetition
of words and phrases helps early readers learn new words. This book also introduces early
readers to subject-specific vocabulary words, which are defined in the Glossary section.
Early readers may need assistance to read some words and to use the Table of Contents,
Glossary, Read More, Internet Sites, and Index sections of the book.

Printed in the United States of America in North Mankato, Minnesota.
042016   009742R

Table of Contents

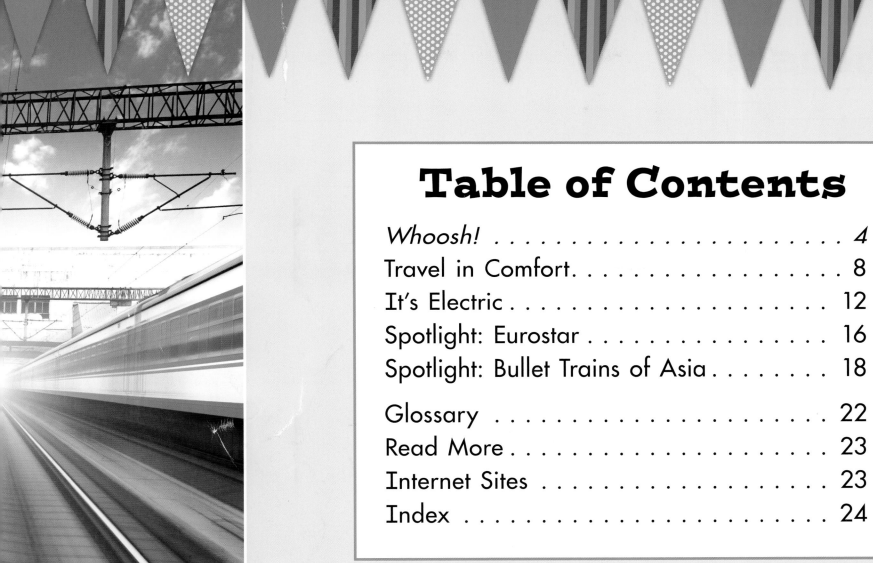

Whoosh!

The platform is full.

You hear a quiet *whoosh*.

A long white car appears.

The high-speed train is here!

High-speed trains whisk riders between large cities. They travel at 125 miles (200 kilometers) per hour or faster. All aboard!

Travel in Comfort

High-speed trains are clean and comfortable. They have restrooms and dining cars. Business travelers can plug in their computers.

Today there are high-speed
trains in Europe and Asia.
The United States and
Canada are planning to
have them too.

a high-speed train
in France

It's Electric

High-speed trains run
on electricity. Special tracks
help them move quickly.
Maglev trains use magnets
to float above the track.

Many people choose between high-speed trains and airplanes. These two vehicles compete to keep travel times and prices low.

Spotlight: Eurostar

The Eurostar travels from London to Paris in 2 hours and 20 minutes. It goes in a 30-mile (50-km) tunnel under the English Channel.

Eurostar Route

London

English Channel

Paris

Spotlight: Bullet Trains of Asia

Japan's high-speed trains are called bullet trains because they are so fast. E5 and E6 bullet trains can go 200 miles (322 km) per hour.

The world's fastest train is the maglev in Shanghai, China. It can rush along at 268 miles (431 km) per hour.

GLOSSARY

car—one of the wheeled vehicles that are put together to form a train

compete—to try hard to outdo others

electricity—a natural force that can be used to make light and heat or to make machines work

high-speed train—a train that travels at a speed of 125 miles (200 km) per hour or faster

maglev train—a train that uses magnets to glide above the track

magnet—a material or object that creates an area of electrical currents that affects other objects

platform—a raised, flat surface; people stand on platforms to wait for trains

track—a rail or set of rails for vehicles such as trains and trolleys to run on

whisk—to move or carry quickly

vehicle—something that carries people or goods from one place to another

READ MORE

Graham, Ian. *Bullet Trains.* Fast! Irvine, Cal.: QEB Pub., 2010.

Riggs, Kate. *Bullet Trains. Seedlings.* Mankato, Minn.: Creative Education, 2015.

Shields, Amy. *Trains. National Geographic Readers.* Washington, D.C.: National Geographic, 2011.

INTERNET SITES

FactHound offers a safe, fun way to find Internet sites related to this book. All of the sites on FactHound have been researched by our staff.

Here's all you do:

Visit *www.facthound.com*

Type in this code: 9781491460399

Check out projects, games and lots more at
www.capstonekids.com

INDEX

Word Count: 187
Grade: 1
Early-Intervention Level: 19